Digital Citizenship

CORWIN
CONNECTED
EDUCATORS
SERIES

The Edcamp Model: Powering Up Professional Learning
By the Edcamp Foundation @EdcampUSA

Worlds of Making: Best Practices for Establishing a Makerspace for Your School
By Laura Fleming @LFlemingEDU

Using Technology to Engage Students With Learning Disabilities
By Billy Krakower @wkrakower and Sharon LePage Plante @iplante

Leading Professional Learning: Tools to Connect and Empower Teachers
By Thomas C. Murray @thomascmurray and Jeffrey Zoul @Jeff_Zoul

*Empowered Schools, Empowered Students: Creating Connected and
     Invested Learners*
By Pernille Ripp @pernilleripp

Blogging for Educators: Writing for Professional Learning
By Starr Sackstein @mssackstein

Principal Professional Development: Leading Learning in the Digital Age
By Joseph Sanfelippo @Joesanfelippofc and Tony Sinanis @TonySinanis

The Power of Branding: Telling Your School's Story
By Tony Sinanis @TonySinanis and Joseph Sanfelippo @Joesanfelippofc

Confident Voices: Digital Tools for Language Acquisition
By John Spencer @spencerideas

The Educator's Guide to Creating Connections
Edited by Tom Whitby @tomwhitby

The Relevant Educator: How Connectedness Empowers Learning
By Tom Whitby @tomwhitby and Steven W. Anderson @web20classroom

Digital Citizenship

A Community-Based Approach

Susan M. Bearden

CORWIN
A SAGE Publishing Company

A SAGE Publishing Company

FOR INFORMATION:

Corwin

A SAGE Company

2455 Teller Road

Thousand Oaks, California 91320

(800) 233–9936

www.corwin.com

SAGE Publications Ltd.

1 Oliver's Yard

55 City Road

London EC1Y 1SP

United Kingdom

SAGE Publications India Pvt. Ltd.

B 1/I 1 Mohan Cooperative Industrial Area

Mathura Road, New Delhi 110 044

India

SAGE Publications Asia-Pacific Pte. Ltd.

3 Church Street

#10–04 Samsung Hub

Singapore 049483

Library of Congress Cataloging-in-Publication Data

Names: Bearden, Susan, author.

Title: Digital citizenship / Susan Bearden.

Description: Thousand Oaks, California : Corwin/A SAGE Company, 2016. | Series: Corwin connected educators series | Includes bibliographical references and index.

Identifiers: LCCN 2015048502 | ISBN 9781483392653 (pbk. : alk. paper)

Subjects: LCSH: Civics—Study and teaching—United States. | Citizenship—Study and teaching—United States. | Political participation—Technological innovations—United States. | Community and school—United States.

Classification: LCC LC1091 .B385 2016 | DDC 370.11/5—dc23 LC record available at http://lccn.loc.gov/2015048502

This book is printed on acid-free paper.

Acquisitions Editor: Ariel Bartlett

Editorial Assistant: Andrew Olson

Production Editor: Amy Schroller

Copy Editor: Deanna Noga

Typesetter: C&M Digitals (P) Ltd.

Proofreader: Dennis W. Webb

Cover and Interior Designer: Janet Kiesel

Marketing Manager: Lisa Lysne

Certified Chain of Custody
Promoting Sustainable Forestry
www.sfiprogram.org
SFI-01268

SFI label applies to text stock

16 17 18 19 20 10 9 8 7 6 5 4 3 2 1

Contents

Preface

My best friend is a high school math teacher. When I started working on the Corwin Connected Educators series, I excitedly told her about the power of using social media to connect with other educators. I passed on what I learned from the authors in this series: that the greatest resource educators have is each other. At a conference, she heard Jennie Magiera speak and finally made the leap to getting on Twitter. Although I wasn't sure she would continue tweeting, she did, and even joined Twitter chats like #connectedtl and #slowmathchat. A few days later, she texted me saying, "I seriously cannot thank you enough. You have changed my life."

Being "connected" seems deceptively simple: Just get on Twitter, right? But that's really not enough. For those who truly embrace connectedness, it's a lifestyle change, an openness to sharing and learning in an entirely new environment. We're seeing the impact of this shift in mindset worldwide. Policies are changing, new jobs in education are being created, hitherto impossible collaborations are happening, pedagogy is evolving, and there's a heightened awareness of each person's individual impact. All of these changes are explored in the Connected Educators series.

While you can see the full list of books on the series page, we're introducing several new books to the series—published in the fall of 2015 and spring of 2016. These books each contribute something unique and necessary not only for educators who are new to the world of connected education, but also for those who have been immersed in it for some time.

Tom Whitby, coauthor of *The Relevant Educator,* has brought together a group of experienced connected educators in his new book, *The Educator's Guide to Creating Connections.* Contributors Pam Moran, George Couros, Kyle Pace, Adam Bellow, Lisa Nielsen, Kristen Swanson, Steven Anderson, and Shannon McClintock Miller discuss the ways that connectedness has impacted them and the benefits it can have for all educators—policy makers, school and district leaders, and teachers.

While all connected educators are evangelists for being connected, connectedness does not necessarily prevent common problems, such as isolation in leadership. In *Breaking Out of Isolation,* Spike Cook, Jessica Johnson, and Theresa Stager explain how connectedness can alleviate the loneliness leaders can feel in their position and also, when used effectively, help leaders maintain balance in their lives and stay motivated.

For districts and schools embracing the connected mindset and empowering all of their learners to use technology, a solid plan for digital citizenship is a must. In *Digital Citizenship,* Susan M. Bearden provides a look at how leaders can prepare teachers and students for the new responsibilities of using technology and interacting with others on a truly global platform.

Connected education provides unique opportunities for teachers in their classrooms as well. In *Standing in the Gap,* Lisa Dabbs and Nicol R. Howard explore the ways that social media can specifically help new teachers find resources, connect to mentors, and encourage each other in their careers. Robert W. Dillon, Ben Gilpin, A. J. Juliani, and Erin Klein show how teachers can purposefully integrate technology and empower their students in both physical and digital classrooms in *Redesigning Learning Spaces.*

One of the most powerful impacts connected education can have is in reaching marginalized populations. In *Confident Voices,* John Spencer shows how social media and other technology tools can empower English language learners. Billy Krakower and Sharon LePage Plante have also discovered that technology can reach special and gifted learners as well.

The books in the Corwin Connected Educators series are supported by a companion website featuring videos, articles, downloadable forms, and other resources to help you as you start and continue your journey. Best of all, the authors in the series want to connect with *you!* We've provided their Twitter handles and other contact information on the companion website.

Once you've taken the step to joining a network, don't stop there. Share what you're doing; you never know when it will help someone else!

—*Peter DeWitt, Series Editor*
@PeterMDeWitt

—*Ariel Bartlett, Acquisitions Editor*
@arielkbartlett

Acknowledgments

If it takes a village to help our students become good digital citizens, it also takes a village to write a book about digital citizenship! I am indebted to so many who helped me on my own digital citizenship journey and paved the way for this book to be written.

Thank you to Dr. Mike Ribble and Jason Ohler, whose books on digital citizenship are a must read for anyone wanting to learn more about the subject; to Dr. Marialice Curran, whose passion for digital citizenship is an inspiration; to Anne Lahr, Brad Meyer, Dr. Joan McGettigan, and Jen Scheffer, for allowing me to share their stories; and to Katrina Stevens, who suggested I write a book in the first place!

I am deeply indebted to the wonderful staff at Corwin, especially to Acquisitions Editor Ariel Bartlett, without whose patience and feedback this book would not have been written. Thanks also to Copy Editor Deanna Noga and Project Editor Amy Joy Schroller.

And finally, thank you to Dr. Kelly Mendoza, the Director of Professional Development, Common Sense Education, who provided insightful and invaluable feedback on the initial manuscript and who has done so much to advance the cause of digital citizenship education.

About the Author

Susan M. Bearden is the Director of Information Technology at Holy Trinity Episcopal Academy in Melbourne, Florida. A former teacher, she frequently presents about social media, education technology, and digital citizenship at national and state conferences including International Society for Technology in Education (ISTE), Future of Education Technology Conference (FETC), the Consortium for School Networking (CoSN), Miami Device, and the Digital Citizenship Summit. In 2015, she was named to the Center for Digital Education's list of "Top 30 Technologists, Transformers and Trailblazers" and received the "Making IT Happen" Award from the Florida Society for Technology in Education. In 2014, she received the Bammy Award for School Technologist of the Year and was a finalist in the education talk show host category.

Bearden cofounded and moderates the #edtechchat and #digcit (digital citizenship) Twitter chats, which are weekly online discussions about education technology and digital citizenship. She is a regular contributor to the popular EdTechChat Radio broadcast for the BAM Radio Network (www.bamradionetwork.com/edtechchat). A popular guest blogger, she has written for a variety of online publications including the Huffington Post, SmartBrief on Education, and Edsurge, and was named one of Common Sense Education's Favorite Digital Citizenship Bloggers to Follow in 2014. Inspired by her experiences with Twitter, she developed Tweechme, a mobile app specifically designed to teach educators how to build Personal Learning Networks on Twitter. Connect with her on Twitter @s_bearden and @Tweechmeapp or at www.susanmbearden.com.

This book is dedicated to my husband, Christopher Bearden, whose encouragement and support knows no limits; and to my father, Roger A. Morrissette, a lifelong educator who dedicated his life to helping children and making the world a better place.

What Is Digital Citizenship?

This is a question that I hear frequently, whether I am talking to students, teachers, administrators, friends, or family members. Digital citizenship can be a confusing topic to the uninitiated, and often it means different things to different people. Cyberbullying is often the first thing that jumps to mind as a common and well-publicized scourge; Internet safety is another. However, digital citizenship is not just about cyberbullying or Internet safety; it encompasses a broad range of behaviors and skills needed in today's digital environments. In his excellent book, *Digital Citizenship in Schools*, Mike Ribble defines *digital citizenship* as "the norms of appropriate, responsible behavior with regard to technology use." The umbrella of digital citizenship covers a broad array of digital literacies, some better known than others, but all important for success in the digital age.

There are some educators who believe that we should take the "digital" out of digital citizenship and just call it "citizenship." And indeed, digital citizenship often goes (and in my opinion, should go) hand in hand with character education. The principles of good citizenship are the same online as they are offline. The online world, however, presents some context-specific challenges that the offline world does not. The anonymity of many social media apps encourages students and adults alike to say and do things online that they would never say face-to-face. Thoughtless posts and inappropriate photos and videos can quickly spread far and wide, viewable by a public audience, at a scale not possible before the advent of social media. The permanency of content posted online—once it's online, it's always online!—means that adolescent mistakes that once "stayed in high school" can haunt students for years to come. Adolescent conflicts and bullying that once stopped at the schoolyard door continue unabated 24/7 because students are constantly connected via cell phones. The relative ease with which students can access inappropriate content (intentionally or not) forces parents and educators to address disturbing social issues at increasingly younger ages. The digital-age culture of oversharing information on social media heightens the importance of teaching children to set appropriate personal boundaries. So while digital citizenship should definitely be viewed as an extension of offline behavior, it is also important to recognize the factors that make it more complex.

The same blurred boundaries between work, school, and home created by the advent of cell phones and our "constantly connected" society are what make a whole community approach to digital citizenship so important. Students are not the only ones who need educating! Parents and educators alike are often equally in need of digital citizenship training. Most of them grew up in a different era, before the advent of these digital tools, and have no previous experiences or role models to guide them in navigating the challenges posed by raising children in the digital age. They may themselves struggle with some of the same online challenges that children do, whether that be social exclusion, cyberbullying, understanding appropriate online etiquette, navigating privacy settings, or feeling societal pressure to be "always available" via cell phone. Adults who don't know how to handle the challenges they themselves face are hardly in a position to help children acquire these skills. At the same time, they may also be unaware of the fantastic learning opportunities provided by the thoughtful use of these same tools, which allow students to connect, collaborate, and learn from students and adults across the country or around the world. Given both the unprecedented challenges and opportunities presented by the digital age, it is clear that digital citizenship education is not solely "the school's responsibility" or "the parent's responsibility," but is instead a community responsibility. Schools are uniquely positioned to spearhead and support such community-based initiatives, and fortunately there is a wealth of online resources designed to help educators take up the challenge.

One of my favorite resources for educators and parents wanting to learn more about digital citizenship is Common Sense Education (www.commonsensemedia.org/educators). Common Sense is a nonprofit organization dedicated, in their words, to "helping kids thrive in a world of media and technology." In addition to providing independent age-based and educational ratings and reviews for movies, games, apps, TV shows, websites, books, and music, they offer additional resources for parents and educators wanting to educate themselves about the perils and incredible opportunities presented by raising children in the digital age. They also offer a suite of free digital citizenship resources for educators, including a free K–12 curriculum. The curriculum is divided into eight separate categories that, along with the curricular framework, were developed based on Howard Gardner's Project Good Play's research on the "ethical faultlines" young people were falling into based on their research. (Links to the research and the Common Sense Education curriculum can be found on the companion website for this book.) These categories may serve as a helpful primer to help answer the question: What is digital citizenship?

INTERNET SAFETY

Internet safety is a core component of digital citizenship. It is often narrowly viewed through the lens of protecting children from predators; children need to learn how to safely navigate an online world in which people can easily pretend to be someone who they are not. Revealing too much personal information can leave children vulnerable not just to predators, but also to identity thieves and other criminals. Location-based "check-ins" and posting geotagged photos online also pose risks. However, Internet safety also includes teaching students how to handle any online situations that make them feel uncomfortable, including exposure to inappropriate material, cyberbullying, and unsolicited approaches from strangers on social networks. Given that students are navigating online spaces at increasingly young ages—I was shocked to discover my 6-year-old granddaughter deftly navigating her way around YouTube!—this training needs to begin as early as kindergarten. It's also important to teach children to balance the risks of Internet use with the rewards, such as being able to communicate and collaborate beyond classroom walls, create and share content, and have their voices heard by a broader audience—not just their teacher and classmates. The online world presents incredible opportunities as well as risks, and a balanced digital citizenship program teaches students about both.

PRIVACY AND SECURITY

Identity theft is a growing problem, with online data breaches being a frequent cause. In a world where even major corporations are hacked on a regular basis, a solid understanding of online privacy and security is an essential life skill. In addition to the risks presented by viruses and malware, Internet users are increasingly vulnerable to e-mail or texting spam and phishing attacks. Poor password habits are common among adults and students—whether that be using simple passwords, sharing passwords with friends, or reusing passwords on multiple sites.

The increasing sophistication of Internet scammers and hackers make it all the more imperative that students (and adults!) learn the basics of online security and how to safeguard their personal information. And with students active in online spaces as young as elementary school, it is increasingly important that they understand what information they should and should not share in online spaces.

In addition to the security risks above, many people are unaware the mere act of browsing the Internet or using a cell phone presents privacy risks. The rise of targeted advertising—whereby Internet ads appear in a user's web browser or mobile device based on their browsing history, product purchases, or other data points—has created a huge market for companies doing business in the buying and selling of our personal data. Mobile device apps are infamous for collecting and sharing user data with third parties and are often riddled with security vulnerabilities. Many free apps—including "educational" and gaming apps popular with children—contain in-app advertising. Privacy policies—which many users don't even bother to read—are often vaguely worded, overly broad, and allow for the collection of far more personal data than is necessary for functional app use. Social media platforms like Facebook are not "free"—the personal data we willingly provide while using these platforms is used to deliver targeted ads as part of the "enhanced user experience." Often, it is a case of balancing the trade-off between personal privacy and convenience. Educated consumers may choose to share some personal data to reap the benefits of technology use. However, students must be taught about how targeting advertising works and the risks that the associated data mining present to their personal privacy. They should understand the importance of customizing privacy settings and how they can do so in web browsers and on mobile devices. They need explicit instruction in understanding privacy policies and how to opt-out of third party sharing. By educating our students about the privacy risks inherent in web browsing and mobile app use, we empower them to make educated choices based on an understanding of the implications.

RELATIONSHIPS AND COMMUNICATION

Two of the biggest relationship challenges created by online communications are (1) written words can be easily misinterpreted in the absence of body language, and (2) people say things online—especially anonymously—that they would never say face-to-face. Learning to communicate respectfully and appropriately online—whether via e-mail, text message, or in other online spaces—is an often overlooked but very important skill. Sadly, it is one that many adults lack! Composing an e-mail to a college admissions officer or potential employer is very different from texting a friend, but students don't necessarily learn this on their own—these are skills that need to be actively taught. Learning how to handle differences of opinion in online spaces is equally important. Whether it be learning how to write a respectful comment on a blog post or collaborative document, or understanding how to deescalate digital drama (recognizing, for instance, that flaming text wars are not an appropriate way to handle conflict), relationship management and communication skills are of paramount importance for students of all ages. It's also important for students to learn how to set boundaries in their digital lives. These boundaries can range from balancing screen time with offline activities, understanding basic digital etiquette (for instance, recognizing that in many social situations it is not polite to pull out a cell phone during a face-to-face conversation), and even understanding how to handle pressure from peers to respond immediately to text messages.

While the digital world can present challenges for relationship management, it can be an incredibly powerful tool for connecting with others. Online spaces make it easy for students to collaborate on projects—whether working with classmates or with students around the world! Video conferencing platforms like Skype or Google Hangouts make face-to-face communication possible at no cost, aside from an Internet connection and bandwidth. Collaborative social media platforms—be they Google Apps for Education, Edmodo, or Twitter—create opportunities for both synchronous and asynchronous communication and collaboration. Twitter hashtags like #comments4kids make it possible for students of all ages to share their work with a worldwide audience and get feedback. It is incumbent upon educators to teach students how to leverage the power of these platforms in an increasingly "flattened" globalized world.

Cyberbullying

If there are school administrators who have not had to deal with cyberbullying in their schools I personally have yet to meet them. The rise of the Internet has made cyberbullying much more pervasive and damaging than the schoolyard conflicts of the past. Adding to the challenges faced by school administrators is the fact that cyberbullying activity often happens after school hours (blurring the boundaries between discipline responsibilities at home vs. school) and the fact that the apps and platforms used for cyberbullying are constantly changing. (Facebook, ask.fm, Kik, Instagram, Yik Yak, and YouTube are just a few that come to mind as of this writing.) The changing technologies can make cyberbullying difficult to recognize and track for adults unfamiliar with the technology landscape frequented by today's students. Although the minimum age for using many of these social media platforms is 13, many younger students are active on these platforms, with or without parent knowledge or consent. This makes cyberbullying education critical even in elementary school.

Teaching students conflict management skills (both online and off) can help reduce cyberbullying. Students need to learn what constitutes cyberbullying (sometimes, a misinterpreted digital communication can blow up into something much worse) and how to react to it, whether they are a bystander or victim. Students can learn how to deescalate online cruelty and be an "upstander" who speaks up and supports and protects someone who is being hurt. It's also important to help parents understand, recognize, and respond to cyberbullying, whether their child is the perpetrator or the victim. They need to be able to recognize potentially dangerous situations that should involve law enforcement, such as threats, as opposed to situations that can be handled with conflict resolution. Many parents want to help their children but don't know how, which is why a successful cyberbullying education program involves the entire school community.

DIGITAL FOOTPRINTS AND REPUTATION

What do you find when you google your name? We live in an age where one's online reputation can seriously impact employment and college prospects. Sadly, many students (and adults!) are oblivious to the impact their online activities have on their digital footprint. Social media sites are heavily indexed by search engines and often appear among the top results. Students often post inappropriate content on social media sites that can easily be accessed with a web search. An increasing number of college admissions officers, coaches, and employers are googling candidate names to determine if they are a good fit for their organization. Business is booming for companies such as Reputation.com and regainyourname.com, which offer services that will, for a fee, help with online reputation management. There are even companies like Social Assurity that specialize in evaluating the digital footprints of college-bound students and helping them clean up their online reputation before applying to college. Digital footprints, for better and for worse, are a reality of the Internet age.

It's worth mentioning that parents are often the first creators of a child's digital footprint. A 2014 study by security firm AVG found that a child's digital footprint can begin before birth, with 30% of parents sharing ultrasound images online. Photos and videos of children shared on social media sites such as Facebook, Instagram, and Flickr start forming their digital footprints long before they are themselves posting content online. While this social sharing often has benefits (such as keeping family and friends up to date on a child's activities), it is often done without understanding the potential future implications. (Will that embarrassing photo be appreciated when the child gets older?) Once again, parent education and awareness are key.

It's important to remember that social media can play a key role in creating a positive digital footprint, not just a neutral or negative one! The digital age provides students (and educators) with unprecedented opportunities to showcase academic and professional work, extracurricular and volunteer activities, and other things that they are proud of. Blogs and other social media sites can help students develop a positive, authentic personal brand and help them connect with recruiters, industry experts, and potential employers. Digital footprints and online reputation management is one area where educators can and should be active role models for our students, parents, and the broader school community. We discuss ways to do this in later chapters.

SELF-IMAGE AND IDENTITY

Searching for identity is an important part of childhood and adolescence. In the digital age, the Internet serves as a "stage" for children to represent themselves. While the digital world can provide healthy outlets for children to explore different identities, it also poses risks. Children are often influenced by mass media (including celebrities, sexualized online content, and the societal representation of gender roles) in how they "think" they should be, look, and act. They post images, comments, and content that often reflects the persona they want to present to the world. However, this online identity doesn't necessarily represent the multifaceted and complex nature of identity. In addition, content posted online can leave students open to cyberbullying or encourage them to engage in other unhealthy behaviors. This makes it all the more important for students to learn how to cultivate positive online identities and relationships. As Alec Couros asked in his 2015 TedXLangley presentation *Identity in the Digital World*: "How do we help our kids discover and experience the many emerging possibilities for networked, human connection while allowing them to safely grow and shape their identities, and the identities of others?"

INFORMATION LITERACY

What does it mean to be literate in the digital age? Whether we are teaching students to evaluate the content and the credibility of online resources or helping them learn effective Internet searching (including advanced search operators), the ability to sift through the vast quantities of information available on the Internet, identify and curate what is valuable, and share it with others is a vital 21st-century skill. The old joke "I read it on the Internet, so it must be true" exemplifies the need to teach students criteria for evaluating and rating online content sources. When it comes to accuracy and veracity, all online sources are most definitely not created equal. It's also important for students and adults to understand how Internet marketing works and how it influences Internet searches. Examples include sponsored links (Internet advertisements that appear in response to specific Internet searches) and browser cookies, which are used to personalize the information that appears in search results according to the user's previous browsing habits. An example of this phenomenon would be of two individuals separately doing online research about a hotly debated political topic. A person who has spent a lot of time browsing conservative news sites will be served up search results that align with conservative political leanings, while the opposite is true for the individual who has previously browsed liberal news sites. Understanding how these processes work (and how to circumvent them) is a critical 21st-century skill.

CREATIVE CREDIT AND COPYRIGHT

The ease of plagiarizing sources in the digital age has spawned services like www.turnitin.com that use computer algorithms to identify content plagiarized from other Internet sources. However, it is not just academic papers where plagiarism and copyright infringement can be found! Many educators do not well understand or model the principles of copyright. They may fail to properly cite an image source in their own presentations, for example, or inappropriately distribute copyrighted textbook materials to their students. They may interpret fair use (which provide educators and work contained in educational settings with specific rights) overly broadly or conservatively, negatively impacting their own use of digital tools in the classroom. (This book's companion website has links to educator guidelines about fair use.) They may not understand the difference between using copyrighted music as background music in a video (which would not be considered fair use) as opposed to remixing the original content in a way that provides social commentary on a topic of class discussion (which would be an example of fair use). Educators who are not comfortable with the principles of copyright and fair use are hardly positioned to guide their students in becoming media literate citizens.

In addition to helping students understand when and how to make use of traditionally copyrighted materials under fair use guidelines, educators need to teach students how to leverage both public domain content and content licensed through Creative Commons. (Creative Commons allows content creators to specifically license their work for public use under specific conditions.) Students should be educated about their rights as content creators and how they can use Creative Commons to license their own work. Because we live in an era where the ease of online information sharing makes copyright infringement (inadvertent or not) as simple as clicking a button, it is critical for educators and students to understand both their rights and the rights of others. The ethical and legal ramifications make an understanding of creative credit and copyright a critical 21st-century skill.

Now that we have outlined the basics of digital citizenship, let's discuss the benefits of teaching it using a community-based approach!

BOOK STUDY QUESTIONS

1. How literate do you consider yourself in each of the eight digital citizenship categories listed above?
2. What would be the benefit to you personally of becoming more literate about digital citizenship?
3. What would be the benefits of implementing a digital citizenship education program in your school or district?

CHAPTER 2

Why a Community-Based Approach to Digital Citizenship?

I n many schools, digital citizenship education is limited both in scope and audience. The focus may be on meeting the minimum requirements for Children's Internet Protection Act (CIPA) compliance, with parent or educator training being a distant consideration. The responsibility for digital citizenship training may lay on the shoulders of a single teacher, perhaps a computer/technology teacher, using a curriculum that meets the CIPA compliance minimum standards but little else. It may be limited to one-off school assemblies that address a narrow facet of digital citizenship, such as Internet safety. "Digital citizenship education" may just be seen as another checkbox to be filled on a lengthy list of state or federal mandates, as opposed to being incorporated into the fabric of the broader curriculum and school culture. With so many standardized tests and pressures faced by educators today, why should schools take on yet another responsibility?

- - - - - - What Is CIPA?

The Children's Internet Protection Act, or CIPA, requires schools that receive government funds for Internet infrastructure to have web filtering solutions in place to protect children from pictures that are (a) obscene, (b) child pornography, or (c) harmful to minors. It also requires schools to have Internet safety policies that include monitoring the online activities of minors and "provide for educating minors about appropriate online behavior, including interacting with other individuals on social networking websites and in chat rooms, and cyberbullying awareness and response."

Although CIPA does not apply to teachers, some schools and districts interpret the legislation very conservatively and end up blocking large swaths of the Internet for students and educators alike. Unfortunately, this often includes many sites with legitimate educational purposes, including YouTube, blogs, wikis, and other social media platforms.

It's worth noting that no Internet filter is foolproof and that determined students will always find a way to get around them. While writing this paragraph, I did a Google search for "Get around web filter" and it turned up over 81,700,000 results! That's not including the students with cellular data plans, which bypass web filters completely.

Complicating the landscape is that schools and districts often struggle with where to set boundaries regarding student behavior online, especially when incidents happen off campus, outside school hours, and not using school equipment. Where do schools draw the line? School responses to this ambiguity vary widely—from administrators who hire companies to actively monitor student social media use, to those who shy away from disciplining students for virtually any off-campus activities. Whose responsibility is it to teach kids about appropriate online behavior anyway? Shouldn't this be a parent responsibility? Why should it be the school's responsibility? In many schools and districts, concerns about these boundaries and the potentially negative impacts of social media may lead to complete bans on its use in educational settings. Extremely restrictive web filtering, often brought on by conservative interpretations of CIPA, is common in many schools. While these concerns are understandable, in practice this philosophy deprives children of the opportunity to learn how to use online tools appropriately and safely, under the guidance of a caring teacher. Instead, many students go from extremely limited access to digital tools during the school day to completely unfiltered Internet access on their cell phones as soon as the bell rings. As Kevin Honeycutt notably observed, our children are out on the digital playground, but no one is watching.

While the philosophical debate over these boundaries rages, the reality is that today's digital technologies present both risks and opportunities. The risks are often better publicized, with cyberbullying, sexting, and online exploitation being the most common ones trumpeted by news headlines. But as Common Sense Education's Kelly Mendoza has said, "the benefits of learning to create, communicate, and collaborate in digital spaces responsibly and safely are the essence of digital citizenship." It is incumbent on educators to help students and parents understand both sides of the equation, to help them leverage the opportunities presented by the online world while educating them about the potential risks. And while any digital citizenship education is better than nothing, the most successful programs weave digital citizenship lessons into the regular curriculum, with an eye toward educating the entire school community.

It's unfortunate that in today's world our students have no shortage of terrible role models when it comes to appropriate behavior in online spaces. Every day, a politician, sports figure, or celebrity courts controversy and career destruction with an obnoxious tweet, a scandalous text, or an embarrassing photo posted online. The comment section on almost any news website is a testament of how low the standards for civil discourse online have become. Adult cyberbullies can be as cruel as adolescent ones. And sadly, parents and even educators can sometimes be included among these poor role models. When facing such seemingly insurmountable challenges, it might be tempting for schools to wash their hands of their responsibility for digital citizenship education beyond the minimum requirements necessary for receiving E-Rate funds.

- - - - - - What Is E-Rate?

E-Rate is a federal program that provides schools, school districts, and libraries with federal funds to subsidize the cost of telecommunications, Internet access, and internal connections. All schools receiving E-Rate discounts must comply with the Internet safety educational requirements outlined in CIPA.

But instead of just focusing on the negative aspects of the digital world, what if schools focused on teaching students, educators, and parents about the benefits by promoting responsible use of digital tools and modeling appropriate online behavior through authentic learning experiences that involve the entire school community?

What if, instead of avoiding social media in school altogether or focusing solely on the negative aspects, we teach students how to leverage it to connect in positive ways and build a digital footprint that reflects their best selves rather than their worst? What if we include parents in the conversation?

What if we intentionally teach students conflict management skills, to help them better negotiate disagreements online and off? What if we teach our children to be "upstanders" in the face of online bullying, to stand up for the victims instead of doing nothing?

What if we teach our students about best practices in cybersecurity, so they can educate their fellow students, friends, and family and make the online world safer for everyone?

What if, instead of completely blocking cell phone use in our schools, we teach students when and how to use them appropriately?

What if, instead of viewing parents as part of the problem regarding inappropriate online behavior, we view them as partners and educate them about appropriate behavior in online spaces so they can better help their children?

What if, instead of avoiding the institutional use of social media platforms like Instagram and Facebook, we use them to build relationships with the broader school community and model best practices in social media use?

What if we recognized that if an ounce of prevention is worth a pound of cure, then helping our children be responsible digital citizens is well worth the investment?

One of the biggest challenges faced by educators wanting to teach digital citizenship is that parents, teachers, and school officials often don't know what they don't know. While there will always be parents and educators who are knowledgeable and proactive about teaching children about digital citizenship, many (perhaps a majority) are not. They may be well-intentioned, but uninformed. They may want to help children navigate these digital waters, but lack the knowledge, practical experience, and digital skill sets to do so. When it comes to emerging digital literacies, parents and educators who came of age in an earlier time often lack the necessary frame of reference needed to help children become responsible digital citizens.

It has been my experience, however, that many parents are aware of the gaps in their knowledge (even if they don't specifically know what these gaps are) and are grateful to get information that helps them be better parents and digital citizens themselves. They are often relieved to know that they are not alone in their fears and uncertainties. They may be intimidated by the vast and ever-changing array of digital tools and platforms used by students today. They may struggle with digital life skills themselves— even basic skills like creating secure passwords and understanding social media privacy settings. They may want to talk to students about their digital lives, but not know how to broach the subject. They may allow or even encourage children under 13 to set up social media accounts, without any understanding of Children's

Online Privacy and Protection Act (COPPA) regulations or the broader implications of underage social media use. But every bit of knowledge they gain will enable them to be better parents who can model, discuss, and reinforce the principles of digital citizenship with their children. Knowledge is power, and if it takes a village to raise a good digital citizen, then proactively educating that village multiplies the impact of digital citizenship training a hundredfold.

What Is COPPA?

The Children's Online Privacy and Protection Act, also known as COPPA, requires website and online service providers directed to children under the age of 13 to give notice to parents and get their verifiable consent before collecting, using, or disclosing personal information from children under 13. The reason that the minimum age for most social media sites is 13 is because many website platforms that are targeted toward adults don't want to address the technical and legal hurdles required to be COPPA compliant. COPPA was updated in 2012, and you can learn more about it from the companion website resources for this book.

It's not just the parents who face a steep learning curve: educators, too, need education! They are often no more knowledgeable about issues such as cybersecurity, privacy, copyright, and online reputation management than their students' parents. For every teacher who is knowledgeable about digital citizenship, there are dozens more who are not. Assuming a baseline understanding of digital literacies and good online judgment is usually a mistake for the same reasons we can't make these assumptions about our students or their parents: educators, like students, usually have not had formal or even informal training in these skills.

The good news, however, is that these skills can be learned and knowledgeable educators can be powerful role models for students and parents! Educators and school districts who use social media and other digital tools wisely and incorporate them into instruction can have a powerful influence on their school community. Digital platforms enable teachers and students to connect and collaborate with others, to share and reflect on their learning, and to provide opportunities to highlight student voice. Digital tools allow educators to communicate with parents and share the great things happening in their schools in a way that weekly paper newsletters and press releases never could. Educators who leverage the power of social media to build Personal Learning Networks and collaborate with other professionals are well-positioned to help students learn to use these tools appropriately. However, many teachers don't know how to leverage these technologies to connect, collaborate, and enhance student learning. Educators need to develop these digital literacies themselves before they can help their students and serve as role models. Just as educating parents helps them be better parents, educating teachers makes them better educators who are better able to support their students.

Digital citizenship is not a one shot lesson or assembly on cyberbullying and social media safety, even if many schools currently teach it that way. Digital citizenship needs to be an ongoing conversation, a conversation about how people conduct themselves online and the specific digital literacies that students need to be successful 21st-century citizens. It needs to be woven into the fabric of a school culture to be the most effective, with lessons reinforced by hands-on activities and even opportunities for students to make mistakes in a safe environment under the guidance of mature, caring adults. Regardless of the terminology, the best tool that educators and parents have is open and honest communication with students about the realities of their online lives, whatever their ages. Including parents and teachers as well as students in digital citizenship education helps all stakeholders understand that when it comes to helping our kids, we are all in it together. A community-based approach to teaching digital citizenship can be a powerful relationship-building tool for school communities. Every step we take to educate the village helps all adults in the school community be better role models for our students.

BOOK STUDY QUESTIONS

1. How is your school or district currently approaching digital citizenship education?
2. How would your school or district benefit from taking a community-based approach to digital citizenship education, as opposed to solely focusing on students?
3. What do you perceive as the biggest challenges you face in implementing a community-based approach to digital citizenship in your school or district?

Demonstrating
Leadership

I f you are a school administrator or teacher leader reading this book, congratulations! You have taken the first step into modeling the characteristics of a good digital citizen by educating yourself. Remember, as a "lead learner," you play a critical role in developing a school culture around good digital citizenship. As you read through this chapter, see which ideas resonate with you and which you might be able to start implementing at your school. Set achievable goals for yourself and commit to following through. Building a culture of positive digital citizenship in your school is not just a goal, it is a journey. Every step you take on this journey will help you better educate your school community. In Chapter 7, we discuss ways to build a comprehensive digital citizenship education program for your school or district.

If you are a classroom teacher, you play a key role in helping students become better digital citizens. Never underestimate the impact you can have on your students, school families, and colleagues! You and you alone set the tone for your classroom, and your influence can extend far beyond your classroom walls. Become a digital citizenship teacher-leader for your school! There are tremendous curricular resources available to educate students and assist your own personal growth.

Take these seven steps to begin your journey!

1. EDUCATE YOURSELF ABOUT DIGITAL CITIZENSHIP

Reading this book is an excellent first step! The more you learn about digital literacy and citizenship, the better prepared you will be to support your school community. There are a number of excellent resources in the online companion to this book to help you learn more. Commit to spending 15 minutes a day on your own digital citizenship education. It's worth the investment, both personally and professionally. Pick one of the topic areas in Chapter 1 and review the resources available on this book's companion website. You'll be amazed at how quickly you can apply what you learn. Even better, share what your newfound knowledge with your family and colleagues! There's no better way to cement your understanding than teaching others, whether that be in a formal classroom setting, an informal conversation during a coffee break, or a discussion at the dinner table. Everything you learn about digital citizenship will make you a better parent, educator, counselor, and friend.

2. MODEL GOOD DIGITAL CITIZENSHIP

Are you using social media professionally? If not, it's time to start! Start building a Personal/Professional Learning Network (PLN) using Twitter or other social media platforms. To learn more, read *Connected Leadership: It's Just a Click Away* by Spike Cook, or *The Relevant Educator: How Connectedness Empowers Learning* by Tom Whitby and Steven W. Anderson. Choose one platform, such as Twitter, Edmodo, LinkedIn, or Google Plus—whatever works best for you—and start from there. Create a professional bio with a headshot and start interacting professionally with other educators in online spaces. Comment on industry-related blog posts using your real name. All these platforms have mobile apps, making it easy to stay connected on the go or during short periods of downtime. (I've gotten great ideas from other educators while standing in line at the supermarket!) Twitter is my personal favorite, and it is popular among connected educators, but it is not the only social media platform you can use to build your PLN. By learning how to use social media yourself, you will both improve your professional practice and get a better understanding for how your students are using it (and how they should be using it!). By modeling appropriate social media use, you'll gain credibility with your school community and be better positioned to advise others. Remember, there is no better way to understand how social media platforms work than to use them yourself. Social media is here to stay, and it plays a huge role in the lives of students. You can jump onboard the train and help guide their journey or be blindsided by it.

Social media can also be a great tool for telling your school's story and building relationships with your school community. In addition to using social media for your own professional learning, consider starting a school Facebook page, blog, or Twitter account to share the great things happening at your school! A great resource for this is *The Power of Branding: Telling Your School's Story* by Tony Sinanis and Joseph Sanfelippo. Social media allows you to communicate with parents throughout the school day, resulting in increased transparency and improved home-school relationships. Real-time updates from your mobile phone can have a far greater impact than a printed weekly school newsletter. All the while, you can model positive social media use. It's a win-win scenario!

3. START TALKING ABOUT DIGITAL CITIZENSHIP

It's up to you to start engaging members of your school community in conversations about digital citizenship! Most people don't know what they don't know, and the first step in educating them is familiarizing them with the vocabulary. Host parent round tables where small groups can discuss topics centered on digital citizenship. Talk to teachers about digital citizenship and what it means to them and for their students. Better yet, get the students talking! They have plenty to say about their online lives if we are willing to listen. Common Sense Education has some terrific materials for facilitating parent talks and student panel discussions, including their Connecting Families program, which you can find through the companion website for this book.

Regardless of whether you are a teacher or an administrator, others will take their cues from you. If your students know that digital citizenship is important, they are more likely to rise to the occasion. What you focus on, you will get more of.

4. DON'T ASSUME THAT FACULTY, STAFF, AND PARENTS KNOW WHAT GOOD DIGITAL CITIZENSHIP LOOKS LIKE

It is important to remember that many people don't have a clear idea of what digital citizenship means, or why it is important. Different people (and even different communities) have different expectations of appropriate online behavior. Whatever your school or district's expectations are, make sure they are clearly communicated and understood throughout your school community. While Acceptable or Responsible Use Policies (known as AUPs or RUPs) are important (see the companion website for resources and examples of these policies), it is not enough just to have a policy—make sure that your school- community lives it! And remember, digital citizenship extends beyond social media use. If you have not yet implemented a school- or district-wide digital citizenship education program, take advantage of less formal learning opportunities. Set aside time in a faculty meeting or a professional development day to discuss issues such as copyright and fair use. Ask your IT department to present to faculty about best practices in personal cybersecurity. Have a counselor discuss strategies for handling cyberbullying. Invite your media specialist to talk about information literacy or advanced web search techniques. Leverage the resources within your school to educate faculty, staff and parents, and encourage them to continue the conversations with students.

5. MONITOR YOUR DIGITAL FOOTPRINT, TALK TO YOUR SCHOOL COMMUNITY ABOUT MONITORING THEIRS

If you work in education, you are being googled—by students, by parents, by journalists, by the community at large. Be proactive in creating and monitoring your digital footprint. Professional social media use can go a long way toward building a positive personal brand for you and your school. Remember the frequently repeated adage: If you don't tell your story, someone else will tell it for you—and it probably won't be the version you want told. Having a significant, positive online presence can also help counteract the existence of negative online content by pushing it further down in the search engine results. Just remember, if it is on the Internet it isn't private—so regardless of privacy settings, you should assume that any and all content you post could be viewed by a public audience. A good rule of thumb: If you wouldn't want something broadcast on the evening news, don't post it online—and that includes e-mail and text messaging.

The fastest way to check your digital footprint is to do a web search for your name and see what turns up. (Be sure to clear your browser cookies and cache first to prevent your search results from being influenced by your browsing history.) Use multiple search engines (like Bing) because the results from each search engine will be a bit different. You can also use tools like Google Alerts, Talkwalker Alerts, and Mention to monitor online references to you and your school. (You'll find links to them in the companion website resources for this book.) To set up alerts, enter your search criteria (such as your name or a school name) and enter an e-mail address. These tools will send you an e-mail or otherwise alert you when content about you (or your school) appears online. These are also excellent tools for students and parents to use. Encourage all members of your school community to be aware of and monitor their digital footprint! It's an important life skill.

6. DON'T EXPECT A POSITIVE DIGITAL CITIZENSHIP CULTURE TO HAPPEN IN A VACUUM

Your school's online culture will evolve from its offline culture. Does your school have a character education program or a mission statement that encourages good citizenship? What systems do you currently have in place to help students manage conflict? How do you address bullying offline? Do your faculty and staff feel supported by school leadership? Do you have a good sense for the "pulse" of your school climate? Good digital citizenship stems from a positive school culture. Remember, "one-shot assemblies" can be helpful in creating awareness about digital citizenship but are no substitute for ongoing, sustained activities and healthy dialog about the social issues students and adults face both online and off.

7. ENCOURAGE AND SUPPORT AUTHENTIC LEARNING EXPERIENCES THAT INCLUDE DIGITAL CITIZENSHIP AS A COMPONENT

The best way to help our students become good digital citizens is to incorporate opportunities that teach digital citizenship into daily classroom activities. Unfortunately, some schools block access to most (if not all) social media platforms and other collaborative communication tools. Even "walled garden" communities like Edmodo or Schoology, which allow students to interact with their peers and teachers in a "closed" online environment, are sometimes blocked. Often, these decisions are made by noneducators (such as technology directors) with little to no discussion of the impact on instruction. Even teachers are denied access to online tools; there are many districts that will not even allow teachers to access YouTube.

Unfortunately, this "lock and block" philosophy often deprives students of the opportunity to learn, with adult supervision, how to conduct themselves appropriately in online spaces. How can we expect our students to acquire these critical skills without scaffolding or guidance, and how can we offer students authentic learning experiences if access to these tools is blocked? One analogy I have heard compares learning appropriate online behavior with getting a driver's license. We wouldn't allow students to get a driver's license without actually driving a car under adult supervision, so why do we expect that students will learn to use social media platforms wisely without guidance? While school Internet access is often heavily filtered, many of our students have cell phones that provide them with completely unfiltered Internet access the minute school gets out. This disconnect is a recipe for digital citizenship disasters.

Web tools such as Kidblog, Edmodo, and Google Drive allow younger students to write, collaborate, and build their communication skills within a closed online environment. For older students, social media platforms like Twitter or Wikispaces can allow students to develop appropriate social media skills while learning traditional curricular content. Blogging for a public audience allows students to get feedback from multiple sources; students "up their game" when they know their work will be seen by a broader audience. Digital portfolios can help students create a positive online footprint while serving as formative assessment. We discuss some examples of embedded digital citizenship activities like these in Chapter 5.

One of my favorite real-life digital citizenship stories comes from a colleague who was using Google Apps for Education to practice collaborative writing with her second graders. Her students were using the commenting feature in Google Docs. One day, a boy in her class wrote "You're a poopy head!" as a comment on a shared document. The student responded with something along the lines of, "Well, you're a super poopy head and your writing stinks!" Since the teacher was reviewing the class comments, she quickly discovered the conversation. It turned out that the boys (who were friends) did not realize that their comments were viewable by all the students in their class and their teacher. The incident of course led to a discussion with both the boys and their parents about appropriate online behavior. While my colleague described the incident somewhat sheepishly, I reminded her that the students in her class had learned a valuable lesson that day, one that they were not likely to soon forget. I would much rather they learn that lesson at a young age, in a safe environment, under the guidance if a caring adult mentor. This is far better than learning that lesson at an older age, in a more public space, using language far more offensive than "you're a poopy head!"

BOOK STUDY QUESTIONS

1. What specific steps will you take in the next month to educate yourself about digital citizenship?
2. What specific steps will you take in the next 3 months to educate your school community about digital citizenship?
3. How can you model the principles of good digital citizenship in your daily life?

CHAPTER
4

Educating Faculty and Staff

N o comprehensive digital citizenship program can be complete without providing professional development for faculty and staff. In the next chapter, we discuss student digital citizenship education, but school and district employees need training just as much as students do! Stories of educators being disciplined or losing their jobs for inappropriate behavior online are not uncommon, and schools and districts have been sued for copyright infringement. From a cybersecurity and data privacy perspective, an uneducated workforce creates serious security risks. Having a well-educated workforce not only mitigates risks such as these, but also teaches school employees to serve as positive role models for students and parents and act as brand ambassadors for your school. Digital citizenship education also empowers teachers to leverage online tools to create real-world, authentic learning experiences. No one can teach or model what they don't themselves understand! If it takes a village to raise a good digital citizen, then educating faculty and staff is a critical but often overlooked piece of the puzzle.

We discuss educating students about digital citizenship in Chapter 5, but at a minimum, an employee digital citizenship training program should include

- Clear policies, procedures and training addressing topics including but not limited to
  - Social media (personal and professional use)
  - Copyright and Fair Use
  - Technology Acceptable/Responsible Use (including cybersecurity)
  - Student data privacy
- Training, curriculum, and strategies for educating students about digital citizenship

Let's discuss these areas in detail.

SOCIAL MEDIA USE

One of the challenges schools face when drafting social media policies is that the individuals tasked with writing the policies are not necessarily skilled social media users. This can result in social media policies that are either overly restrictive (which can lead to legal challenges related to First Amendment rights) or too vague. The best policies are flexible documents developed by people who understand how various social media platforms work and can thus identify the risks and benefits. You can find some examples on the companion website resources for this book. It's also important to clearly define what constitutes appropriate social media use for a given community (remember, not everyone has the same interpretation of what constitutes appropriate!) and to update policies as technologies change.

Because social media can blur the boundaries between one's personal and professional lives, it's important to differentiate between professional and personal social media use. For instance, a teacher might create a professional Twitter account or a class blog to communicate with students and parents. This is different from a personal Facebook or Instagram page geared toward family and friends. It's important to clarify the rules of student-teacher interactions in online spaces; employees often have questions about what is and isn't appropriate. For instance, what should a teacher do if they receive a friend request on their personal Facebook page from a student? How about a parent?

It's also important to communicate that privacy settings are not absolute and that content can be shared far beyond the intended audience. As I mentioned earlier, if you work at a school, you are being googled—whether by students, parents, journalists, or other community members. All school employees need to be aware that, right or wrong, they are often held to a higher standard of behavior than people who work in other professions, and therefore need to conduct themselves online accordingly. Encouraging teachers to build Professional/Personal Learning Networks online is a great way to help them understand important digital citizenship concepts such as privacy settings and digital footprints. Professional social media use can help them better understand the implications and influence of content posted online (both positive and negative).

The New York City Department of Education has excellent social media policies for students and employees on their website, which you can find in the companion website resources.

COPYRIGHT AND FAIR USE

Formal training in the area of copyright and fair use is a must in the digital age. Like students, teachers will often appropriate photos, videos, and other digital content into teaching materials without giving thought to copyright. Fair use allows for the limited use of copyrighted material in educational settings without getting permission from the copyright holder, but is often misunderstood by educators. This limits their ability to leverage digital content in creative ways. Educators also need to be educated about their rights as content creators. Many teachers are sharing lesson plans and other teaching materials online; they need to understand their rights as copyright holders, including the ability to license their materials through Creative Commons. Educators who understand their rights as content creators are much better positioned to help students understand theirs. School librarians are often excellent sources of information about copyright and fair use and can help direct teachers to public domain and licensed Creative Commons content.

TECHNOLOGY ACCEPTABLE USE/ RESPONSIBLE USE POLICIES

While most organizations have Acceptable Use Policies (AUPs) governing the use of school or district IT resources, it is helpful to review the policies with faculty and staff as opposed to just burying it in an employee manual. Even better, *involve your school community in writing these policies!* Employees (and students) are much more likely to buy into policies if they have a voice in how they are written. A collaborative approach to developing AUPs will help all stakeholders (IT staff, employees, and students) understand each other's needs and perspectives. This usually results in more flexible policies that balance constituent needs and empowers teachers and students to leverage technology in teaching and learning instead of discouraging them. Some schools are shifting to the term Responsible Use Policies (RUPs), which emphasizes the responsible use of technology, instead of AUPs. The change in wording emphasizes a more collaborative approach between IT departments and the school communities they serve. You can find resources about AUPs and RUPs on the companion website.

Cybersecurity is another area where employee education can reap huge dividends. Teaching educators how to recognize phishing e-mail, create strong passwords, and protect themselves from malware will result in a workforce less likely to behave in ways that put your school's network at risk. While high profile hackers may grab the headlines, the teacher or school secretary who lists their passwords on a sticky note on their desk can be just as dangerous! Many adults are surprisingly unsophisticated in this regard, making proactive approach to cybersecurity education a worthwhile investment. As an added benefit, cybersecurity-savvy teachers are better able to develop cybersecurity-savvy students.

STUDENT DATA PRIVACY

Protecting student data in the digital age is an increasingly important and controversial topic. In today's educational environment, a tremendous amount of student data is collected and analyzed in a variety of software programs, which vary by school and/or district. This information can range from directory information (such as name, address, and phone number) to attendance history, socioeconomic status, disciplinary history, and academic progress. While student data can be a valuable educational tool, enabling educators to identify at-risk students and better differentiate instruction, it can potentially be misused by third parties. As of this writing, there is a tremendous debate at the national level about the importance of safeguarding student data and making sure that it is only used for educational purposes.

The Family Educational Rights and Privacy Act, or FERPA, is a federal law that helps ensure the privacy and accuracy of education records. However, many educators are unfamiliar with FERPA guidelines and can inadvertently violate the law. Many of the digital tools used in instruction may violate FERPA if used without parental consent. It is therefore incumbent upon schools and district to develop policies and procedures surrounding the use of digital tools and educate teachers about these policies.

Kirk Anderson, the Director of Educational Technology for Denver Public Schools, has created an excellent (and humorous) video explaining the district's privacy policies and processes that teachers must follow to ensure that their use of digital tools remains FERPA compliant. You can find a link to the video in the companion web resources for this book.

The Family Educational Rights and Privacy Act law applies to all schools that receive certain federal funds from the U.S. Department of Education. The law gives parents certain rights regarding their children's education records, rights that transfer to the student when he or she reaches the age of 18 or attends a school beyond the high school level. It specifies under what specific circumstances schools can release information from a student's education record without parental consent (i.e., schools to which a student is transferring). It also specifies that students may disclose directory information such as student's name, address, telephone number, and date of birth, but that parents and eligible students (students over 18) must be advised about the directory information and given the opportunity to request that such information not be shared.

In Chapter 7, we discuss some ideas for putting together a comprehensive digital citizenship education program that includes faculty and staff. But first let's discuss ways to educate our core constituents: students!

BOOK STUDY QUESTIONS

1. What are some ways in which you might educate faculty and staff about digital citizenship?
2. What are some of the challenges you face in educating faculty and staff about digital citizenship?
3. What specific steps can you take to overcome these challenges?

Educating Students

E ducating students about digital citizenship is of course the heart of this book. Incorporating digital citizenship lessons organically into the fabric of daily lessons is probably the most effective approach, but as we discussed in the previous chapter, this approach requires teachers to be educated and comfortable with the concepts of digital citizenship first. As Common Sense Education's Kelly Mendoza has noted, effective digital citizenship education also requires educators to take an interest in their students' digital lives and understand the role that digital tools play. While there is no "one size fits all" solution, there are a number of terrific curriculum resources to help teach students about digital citizenship. Several of them can be found in the online resources for this book. Some resources are designed as stand-alone online lessons, others are designed to supplement or be incorporated into the teaching of other academic subjects. The most important step in your journey to educate students about digital citizenship is *to start doing it*! In Chapter 7, we discuss how to put together a comprehensive digital citizenship training program for an entire school or district, but if you aren't in a position to lead a large scale effort, you can still make a difference. Tackle the proverbial elephant one bite at a time: upgrade one unit per semester by incorporating digital citizenship education. Figure out what area your school community most needs help with, or what fits most naturally into your existing curriculum, and start with that. If you are an administrator, identify one or two teachers in your building who you feel might be good "champions" for digital citizenship education and ask them to introduce a lesson or two into their existing curriculum and provide them with all the needed supports. Or jump in and teach a couple of lessons yourself! Every step forward is a step in the right direction. And don't forget to ask your students for input. Engage them in conversation and ask them about their digital citizenship-related concerns. Listen carefully and you'll know where you need to start.

In addition to utilizing a formal digital citizenship curriculum, an important part of digital citizenship education is providing students with opportunities to practice their skills. "Walled gardens" such as Edmodo or Google Apps for Education allow students to develop a "phased" online presence, providing a safer environment for kids to make mistakes (and all mistakes should be viewed as learning opportunities!). For older students, leveraging social media in the classroom can support curriculum, provide quieter students with a "voice," and help students develop positive digital footprints. Here are some examples:

- Have students blog and teach them how to comment appropriately on other blog posts.
- Engage students using online discussion boards using a tool like Edmodo.
- Use Twitter to extend and enhance classroom discussions of English literature.
- Engage authors, scientists, or other business professionals in classroom conversations via Twitter.

There are many other ways to incorporate digital citizenship education within the context of other academic subjects. A few examples might be:

- After a lesson on copyright, assign a PowerPoint presentation that requires proper image citation.
- Before beginning a research paper, have students practice web search skills.
- Ask older students to write and design public service announcements to educate younger students about online privacy.
- Have students create "Fakebook" pages for major historical characters.

The possibilities are limited only by your imagination!

Here are a few examples of schools that have incorporated digital citizenship into their curriculum in a variety of ways:

Holy Trinity Episcopal Academy

A preschool–12 independent school in Melbourne, Florida, Holy Trinity was the first Common Sense Education Digital Citizenship Certified School in the state. Holy Trinity utilizes both the Common Sense Education Digital Citizenship curriculum and other free online resources at both the lower (PS–6) and upper (7–12) schools. At the lower school, digital citizenship lessons are supported by a robust character education program. 21st Century Learning Specialist Brad Meyer (@Brad21CLSMeyer) works closely with classroom teachers and lower school librarian Judy Houser (@jhouser1) to introduce and reinforce digital citizenship lessons throughout the year. Activities range from computer lab sessions that target specific lessons from the Common Sense Education curriculum to more informal opportunities that arise from in-class activities, such as blogging and document sharing using Google Drive. Some of the most effective lessons, says Meyer, are the informal ones, such as those that arise from casual classroom conversations or one-on-one discussions. "Students know that I am always available" to answer questions, he says.

Meyer holds two Common Sense Education certifications: Digital Citizenship Certified Educator and Graphite Certified Educator. Parents are excited that the school has a digital citizenship expert on staff and appreciate the school's proactive approach to teaching digital citizenship. "They are grateful," says Meyer, "that their kids are being taught about digital citizenship in a hands-on way, and that we not just giving the students technology but teaching them how to use it responsibly."

Digital citizenship education needs to start at the elementary level, believes Meyer, and the earlier the better. "You may think it is too early or not necessary, but it is vitally important. Make the time, use whatever resources are at your disposal, and make (conversations about) digital citizenship a part of your daily routine—just like lining up or clean up time. You will be surprised at how much they learn and the long term rewards of this approach."

At Holy Trinity's Upper School, eighth-grade American History teacher Anne Lahr—also a Common Sense Education Digital Citizenship Certified Educator—got started when she decided to broaden her traditional citizenship unit to include digital citizenship. She started with teaching a few lessons from Common Sense's Digital Citizenship curriculum during the first year, then expanded the scope of her digital citizenship training by incorporating Common Sense's "Digital Bytes" program to spark in-class conversations with her students. She also has her students get their "Digital Driver's Licenses" using the University of Kentucky's free online program. A 25-year veteran educator, Anne says that her students have probably been using the Internet "even longer than I have" but emphasizes the need for teachers to adapt to the changing digital landscape. "These are skills that they need. The Internet is a beautiful, wonderful place, but it can also be very dangerous. I think it is more about helping them develop awareness than anything else." The Common Sense Education materials, she said, are flexible enough to work with many different subjects. "You can pick and choose the materials that best align with your other teaching goals."

Lahr begins teaching digital citizenship during the first week of school, starting with a project from the Common Sense Education lesson called "My Digital Life" that has students reflect on the role of digital media in their lives. Students create videos about their digital lives using Animoto and share them with the class. In addition to laying the groundwork for the lessons that follow, the icebreaker activity helps her get to know her students. She then moves on through some of the other lessons during the next week, including those on cyberbullying, information literacy, and creative credit and copyright. Lahr makes a point of asking students to teach her about the apps and tools they use on a regular basis. "I play dumb and the kids love it! They really open up when they feel they are teaching you something. They are so eager to share and teach me how their favorite programs work. You get a real sense of how they are using them and how they fit into the social fabric of their lives."

Lahr recommends that educators new to the concepts of digital citizenship start by exploring the Common Sense Education curriculum from the perspective of a student. "Go through some of the lessons yourself and reflect upon your learning," she recommends. Working through the creative credit and copyright lessons, for instance, made her much more sensitive to potential copyright issues in her own professional practice. Another benefit of going through the lessons, she says, was making connections to material already covered by her history curriculum. This allows her to better leverage the Common Sense material to reinforce her existing lesson content. For example, she connects the creative credit and copyright lessons to the history of patent law. "Patent laws were in the Articles of Confederation, even before the Constitution was written," she said. "Our Founding Fathers understood the importance of protecting people's creative work." Discussing contemporary issues against the background of historical content helps bring history to life in Lahr's classroom.

North Broward Preparatory School

At North Broward Preparatory School, an independent high school in Coconut Creek, Florida, a course in Personal Branding and Digital Communication is a graduation requirement. The trimester class is taught by academic technology teacher Jason Shaffer and is designed to help students learn how to harness the power of social media and understand the importance of cultivating a personal brand online. The idea for the course, according to school's Director of Education and Information Technology, Dr. Joan McGettigan (@drmcgettigan), came about as a way to meet the needs of students facing a changing digital landscape. "Like many high schools, we had a typical 'intro to technology' class covering Office applications," she says. "However, in today's world, that was not very helpful."

Class activities include blogging and setting up accounts on several social media platforms, including Twitter, Instagram, and Google Plus. The focus is on appropriate use and creating a positive digital footprint. Self-reflection is an important element of the course, with students evaluating their strengths and weakness to best craft their "brand." Topics covered in the curriculum also include digital rights and ethics, content curation, and public speaking.

"From a digital citizenship perspective, we want our students to understand the ramifications of poor social media use, but also go beyond that," says McGettigan. "We want our students to be well versed in digital communications and understand the culture specific to different social media platforms. If it is true that the average U.S. citizen will change careers (not just jobs) 8 to 10 times over the course of a lifetime, and that for two or three of those positions you will have to recreate yourself, then it is imperative that students know how to brand themselves. If they don't, someone else will."

According to McGettigan, students not only enjoy the class, but they also thank the instructor for it. Parent response to the course has been positive; most are relieved that the school is addressing issues with which many of them are uncomfortable. "Every year we have a couple of parents who question the need for their child to set up social media accounts as part of the course, but when we educate them about the 'Why' they come to appreciate it. We've also had many parents tell us that they wish we offered a version of the class for them!"

McGettigan is passionate about teaching students appropriate social media use. "Students are carefully coached when learning to drive," she says. "They are taught about the dangers of the road, how to operate and maintain a car, what to do in an emergency, how to park, and how to handle traffic and bad weather. Why don't we do the same thing before letting our students loose in the digital world? They need to understand how to navigate this constantly shifting world safely."

Burlington High School

At Burlington High School (BHS), a public school in Burlington, Massachusetts,, Mobile Learning Coach Jennifer L. Scheffer teaches the Student Technology Innovation and Integration course, a semester-long elective open to students in Grades 10–12. Students in the course run the BHS Help Desk, which provides technical and instructional technology support for teachers and students in their 1:1 iPad program. In addition, the course includes a substantial digital citizenship and digital literacy component, with students leveraging a variety of social media tools as part of their day-to-day classroom activities.

Using a curriculum developed by Scheffer, students learn about digital citizenship through real-world, authentic learning experiences that benefit both the students and the broader school community. Class participants are required to contribute regularly to the BHS Help Desk blog by creating a variety of original digital content including blog posts, presentations, screencasts, app reviews, videos, digital stories, and Google Hangouts on Air. Through contributing to the blog, which has a global audience, students learn the technical aspects of sharing content (embedding multimedia, linking to outside resources, and properly citing and crediting online content) and the legal issues surrounding intellectual property. The BHS Help Desk also has its own YouTube channel, known as Help Desk Live, where students post video interviews with students and industry professionals recorded via Google Hangouts. Guests have included company CEOs, app developers, college professors, K–12 educators, book authors, and other students.

Help Desk students also moderate professional Twitter chats with other educators using the hashtag #TechTeamMA. They have also guest moderated other Twitter chats, including #edtechchat and #digcit. Help Desk students have participated in the #edtechchat radio broadcast on the BAM! Radio Network and have even been invited to present at professional education conferences, including the national Digital Citizenship Summit (CT), EduCon (PA), Mass-CUE (MA), and the Christa McAuliffe Technology Conference (NH).

"Each student completes an online career portfolio," says Scheffer, "including a LinkedIn account, digital resume, and an online profile using a platform like About.me, branded.me, or Flavors .me. Students understand the difference between sharing personal versus professional information and how social media can be used to enhance (or hurt) their future academic and career opportunities." They are also encouraged to use digital tools to connect with industry experts to help them personalize their Help Desk learning experience.

Internet ethics is another important component of the course. "Help Desk students understand privacy settings and how to use digital tools in a safe and ethical way," says Scheffer. Students are taught the types of information they should avoid sharing online as well as how to respond to incidents of cyberbullying, trolling, and other negative online behavior. Scheffer also encourages her students to promote a culture of kindness online and to be "upstanders" in the face of inappropriate online behavior. Due to their effective and ethical use of digital tools, many Help Desk students have emerged as digital role models for other teens.

Scheffer sees digital citizenship and literacy training as a critical component of preparing students for the 21st-century workforce. "My favorite aspect of teaching the course is that students have access to modern digital tools," she says. "This helps them create an authentic digital identity not through simulations, but through real world experiences. They leave the course with an understanding of how to succeed and be competitive both on and offline."

As shown by the examples above, there are many different ways to develop a digital citizenship program at your school. In Chapter 7, we talk about how you develop your own digital citizenship education program. In the next chapter, however, we discuss the importance of educating another important constituency: parents.

BOOK STUDY QUESTIONS

1. What are some ways in which you might incorporate digital citizenship education with your students?
2. What are some of the biggest challenges you face in incorporating digital citizenship education into your curriculum?
3. What specific steps can you take to overcome these challenges?

Educating Parents

Parents play a key role in educating students about digital citizenship. However, one of the challenges schools face in partnering with parents to educate students about digital citizenship is that many parents don't know what they don't know. Parents have differing levels of knowledge and awareness, depending on a variety of factors that include personal experience, socioeconomic status, and parenting styles. Even proactive, educated parents often have large gaps in their understanding of digital citizenship. Thus, parent education plays a critical role in helping our students become good digital citizens.

When today's parents were themselves children, the social media tools so prevalent today did not exist. As a result, parents often have no personal experiences or role models to draw from when it comes to educating their children about appropriate online behavior. Many cultural norms associated with parenting don't necessarily translate to the digital world. As a result, parents usually want to help their children, but they don't always know how. Some parents are completely oblivious to potential online perils, allowing children unsupervised and unfiltered Internet access at young ages. Others are so overprotective that they may object to a teacher using "walled garden" platforms like Edmodo or Schoology with students. It's important to teach parents about both the positive and negative aspects of our digital world. While some schools might prefer to view educating children about digital citizenship as a parent responsibility, the reality is that many parents are not equipped to do so and they are looking to teachers and schools for help. Schools can and should meet parents where they are and be proactive in their approach to parent education.

It's been my experience that many parents are hungry for "digital age" parenting information and grateful for the opportunity to learn more. They are often relieved to hear that other parents share their questions or concerns. And effective parent education sessions do not always have to be formal presentations! Some of the most meaningful parent education sessions I have conducted were round table discussions with a group of parents centered on a particular topic, like cell phones. Questions like, "When is it OK to get my child a cell phone?" and "How can I learn more about their online friends?" are common. Educating parents about digital citizenship and engaging them in honest, open dialog not only makes them better parents but also can serve as a powerful relationship-building tool for teachers and administrators. It's important to remember that you don't have to have all the answers to have a valuable discussion with parents. For instance, check out the Common Sense Education Connecting Families Program listed in the companion website resources. The program is designed so that any facilitator can engage parents in meaningful conversations, even if they do not consider themselves experts on a particular topic.

It's worth mentioning that schools often bring in law enforcement professionals to talk about Internet safety at evening assemblies. While these events can raise awareness, these "one and done" assemblies usually focus on legalities and risk and don't help build parent confidence. Parents are better served by conversations over time that take a balanced approach to the risks and benefits of online tools. It's also important to remember that parent education should not be limited to middle and high school parents. The proliferation of mobile devices means that children are accessing the Internet at increasingly younger ages. It is not uncommon to see preschool-aged children playing on a parent's cell phone. Digital citizenship training for students and parents needs to start in early childhood—kindergarten is not too young to start.

PARENTS AS ROLE MODELS: THE GOOD AND THE BAD

It's an unfortunate reality that our students have no shortage of terrible adult role models when it comes to online behavior. There is a long list of celebrities and politicians whose careers have been derailed by the dumb things they have done on the Internet. Athletes have been sent home from the Olympics, lost scholarships, or been otherwise penalized for a thoughtless tweet. Business professionals have lost their jobs over an insensitive Facebook post. Even more disturbing, however, are the parents who behave inappropriately online. While many do serve as positive role models for their children, others do not. Adults make many of the same mistakes our students do regarding digital media. With such poor role models, is it any surprise to see children behaving the same way? These behaviors make comprehensive parent education an even more important component of any digital citizenship program. Parents need to be reminded that, as in other aspects of parenting, they are their child's first digital citizenship role models. The parents who are glued to their cell phones at the dinner table or who text while driving should not be surprised when their children emulate these behaviors.

WAYS TO INVOLVE AND EDUCATE PARENTS

There are many ways to involve and educate parents about digital citizenship, and no one approach will work for every school community. Use the following ideas as a starting point and modify them to meet the needs of your school. When planning parent training, remember to educate parents about the positive aspects of Internet use as well as the downsides. For instance, many parents don't understand how social media platforms can be used for collaboration on school projects or leveraged to help students build a positive digital footprint.

Parent Coffees and/or Tech Nights

Invite parents to attend presentations or discussions about digital citizenship related topics. For example, the Common Sense Education Connecting Families program offers a wealth of parent resources, including conversation starters, facilitation guides, written materials, and educational videos. If you record or screencast the presentation for parents unable to attend and post it on your school website, you'll reach even more families. By inviting students to participate and/or do some or all the teaching, you are guaranteed an audience!

Share Resources Online

Create a digital citizenship page on your school website. There are many excellent parent education resources on the companion website for you to include. Do you have a school blog? Consider writing about digital citizenship–related topics (or even better, have students write about them). If you don't have a school blog, the Common Sense Education Parent Toolkit has widgets that allow you to embed their parent blog feed on your school website so you constantly have fresh content. Then advertise your website resources!

Create Opportunities
for Students to Teach Parents

Have students create digital citizenship–related projects using digital media. They might create a public service announcement using iMovie, interactive digital posters using Glogster or Thinglink, or even a simple PowerPoint presentation. Then share these presentations with parents! Invite them for a student-led "Digital Citizenship" night, where students share their projects. If you don't host an evening event, post the projects on your school website and invite parents to view their child's work.

Share Information via Text, School Newsletters, or E-Mail

Do you have a weekly school newsletter or e-mail? Why not create a weekly feature with tips about digital age parenting? Does your school have a Facebook page? Share digital parenting resources there as well. Do your school parents frequently communicate via mobile devices? Consider using a service like RemindHQ and invite parents to sign up to receive text messages with links to digital citizenship–related resources topics. You could do the same thing with a Twitter account and encourage parents who are not on Twitter to use Twitter's fast-follow feature to receive these tweets as text messages. (See the companion website for a link to a screencast that demonstrates how to sign up to receive tweets as text messages.) Reach your parents where they are, and don't be afraid to use multiple channels to do so! Some parents will prefer to get a handout brought home by a student, another might prefer to get a text. The important thing is that the more parents hear about digital citizenship, the more likely they are to absorb the message. Experiment with different communication modalities; don't limit yourself to just one. Most important, **don't give up!**

While educators can't control parent behavior, they can take a proactive approach to parent education and serve as positive online role models. Try one of the ideas above and see what works for your specific community. Use social media in a positive, professional manner and model the digital skills we want students (and their parents) to acquire. Whether through a class blog, a professional Twitter feed, or a school Facebook page, engage parents in positive ways through social media. And don't stop talking about it!

At one parent presentation, a mother asked me a question about Clash of Clans, an online game popular among fifth-grade boys at my school. We discussed the importance of monitoring his online interactions with other gamers, and I suggested she ask her son to show her how to play the game so that she could connect with her son's interests and better understand what he was doing. The following month, she came back thanking me profusely for the advice! It turned out that her son had indeed been playing the game with a group of strangers, unaware of the potential risks. She talked with him about the dangers and worked with her son so he was able to continue playing the game with a group of boys he knew in real life. The relief on her face was palpable. I realized that if my presentation had helped even one mother be a better parent and helped one child be safer online, it was worth the time and effort.

By enlisting parents as partners in digital citizenship education, and giving them the information and skills necessary to better help their children, we can greatly expand the effectiveness of our own digital citizenship education efforts. In the next chapter, we discuss how to pull it all together by putting together your own digital citizenship education program.

BOOK STUDY QUESTIONS

1. How would your school or community benefit from including parents in conversations about digital citizenship?
2. What are some of the biggest challenges you face in educating parents?
3. What specific steps can you take to overcome these challenges?

CHAPTER
7

Putting It All Together

Building a Comprehensive Digital Citizenship Program

Having read this far, hopefully you are now sold on the importance of community-based digital citizenship education in your school or district and are ready to take the next step. However, you might be asking, "Where do I begin?" While there is no one way to implement a digital citizenship program, you might find the following guidelines helpful. Common Sense Education's Kelly Mendoza, the Director of Professional Development for Education Programs, recommends schools interested in implementing a digital citizenship program take the following steps:

1. **Identify a digital citizenship lead and bring key stakeholders together to form a project team.** Whether you are looking to implement a digital citizenship program for a school or for an entire district, it is critical to identify an enthusiastic

project leader for your digital citizenship initiative. Stakeholder voice is equally important. Your project team may include teachers, administrators, parents and/or caregivers, and even students. Student voice is often overlooked in the planning phase of digital citizenship initiatives but can bring valuable perspectives to the conversation. Make sure you clarify and communicate expectations for team members: what are their roles on the project team, and for what will they be held responsible?

2. **Develop a digital citizenship vision. Record it.** What do you want your digital citizenship education program to look like? What do you wish your students, teachers, and parent community to understand and do as a result of your initiative? Developing and communicating your digital citizenship vision serves as a guide for implementation and helps you garner community support. The Common Sense Education Digital Citizenship Implementation plan, to which you can find a link in the companion resource website for this book, includes some examples of digital citizenship vision plans in the FAQ section of the document.

3. **Explore education resources and discuss ideas with the team.** The companion website for this book lists a plethora of resources for educating your school community about digital citizenship. Common Sense Education offers a free K–12 Digital Literacy and Citizenship Curriculum that satisfies the criteria for E-Rate compliance and is aligned with Common Core State Standards, the International Society for Technology in Education's National Education Technology Standards (ISTE's NET•S), and the American Association of School Librarians (AASL) Standards. There are other curriculum resources on the companion website as well. See which resources might be the best fit for your school community. It's OK to mix and match based on community needs.

4. **Map out your digital citizenship plan.** Determine how, when, and who will provide digital citizenship instruction to faculty, students, and parents. You may find the Common Sense Education implementation plan helpful; it is included in the companion website resources. Here are some aspects to consider:

   a. **Students**—At what grade levels will instruction occur, how many hours of instruction will there be, and what resources will be used? Will it be incorporated into a specific academic subject? Who will be responsible for providing the training?

b. **Teachers**—How will teachers be trained? Will your training only include teachers involved in direct digital citizenship instruction, or will you expand it to include the broader faculty and staff community? How will you track and evaluate the instruction?

c. **Parents**—How will you engage and educate your school community? What communication strategies and methods will you use?

5. **Communicate your plan and get everyone on board.** A well thought out communications strategy will go a long way to earning community buy-in. It's important for stakeholders to understand the rationale and benefits of implementing a digital citizenship education program. Be sensitive to the time needed for educator training and implementation so that it is not considered just "one more thing" teachers need to do. Ask your project team members how to best frame the conversation so that it is not viewed negatively as a top-down initiative. Enlist the support of educators "in the trenches" to help ensure your message is well-received.

6. **Train Teachers.** If you are interested in using Common Sense media materials, a link to their teacher education resources can be found on the companion website. Some questions to consider: Will you incorporate digital citizenship education into traditional professional development days or use online resources? Is a "train the trainer" approach an effective method of educating your faculty and staff? How can you reward and highlight educators willing to go the extra mile in teaching digital citizenship? How will you track training completion rates? Will your digital citizenship training include noninstructional staff?

7. **Execute your plan, including delivering student instruction and engaging parents.** As you implement your instructional and parent outreach plans, take the time to evaluate your implementation. Get stakeholder feedback (including students) to determine program effectiveness. Make changes as needed to improve or enhance your digital citizenship education

program. View your program as a work in progress and strive to improve it every year!

A few events you may wish to celebrate as part of your digital citizenship initiatives include Digital Citizenship Week (usually held in October of each year) and Safer Internet Day (an international event held in February). A Google search will help you find the dates for a specific year.

STEPS FOR CONTINUED PERSONAL AND PROGRAMMATIC GROWTH

Digital citizenship education is an ongoing process. As technologies change, so will the challenges and opportunities they present. As educators, parents, and citizens of the online world, it is incumbent upon us to stay abreast of changing landscape and commit to our own personal growth. Here are some resources that will help you stay abreast of the latest developments in digital citizenship curriculum, news, and trends (links can be found on the companion website):

1. **Join the ISTE Digital Citizenship Learning Network.** The International Society for Technology in Education has a learning network for individuals interested in digital citizenship education. It's a great way to connect with like-minded colleagues.

2. **Participate in the #digcit Twitter chat and follow the #digcit hashtag on Twitter.** The #digcit Twitter chat is a series of online conversations about digital citizenship held on Wednesdays at 7 pm ET/ 4 pm PT. Participating in the chat or even just searching for the #digcit hashtag on Twitter is a great way to stay abreast of current trends, technologies, and events related to digital citizenship.

3. **Join the edweb.net digital citizenship community.** This free professional learning community provides ideas, discussions, and webinars about digital citizenship. It's a great place to ask questions and share ideas and best practices about teaching digital citizenship.

4. **Common Sense Media.** In addition to the many curricular resources provided by Common Sense Education, the main Common Sense Media website provides a wealth of resources for parents including digital media reviews (movies, books, video games, apps, and more), blog posts on digital citizenship–related topics, family media guides, and more.

CONCLUSION

As educators, parents, and adults who care about the welfare of children, we all hope that our students will grow up to be responsible citizens of the world who contribute to society in constructive ways. In the digital age, that includes positive and healthy participation in online spaces. Educators are uniquely positioned to help students become responsible digital citizens, but as we have previously discussed, digital citizenship education is most effective when implemented as a community effort. So in closing, I encourage you to start building your digital citizenship village today!

BOOK STUDY QUESTIONS

1. If you were charged with putting together a digital citizenship project team for your school or district, who would you select as your project lead and team members? Why would you choose these specific individuals?

2. What do you view as the biggest potential roadblocks to implementing a comprehensive digital citizenship education program at your school or district? How can you overcome these roadblocks?

3. What specific steps will you take as a result of reading this book to facilitate the implementation of a community-based digital citizenship program in your school or district?

A SAGE Publishing Company

Helping educators make the greatest impact

CORWIN HAS ONE MISSION: to enhance education through intentional professional learning.

We build long-term relationships with our authors, educators, clients, and associations who partner with us to develop and continuously improve the best evidence-based practices that establish and support lifelong learning.

Solutions you want. Experts you trust. Results you need.

Author Consulting

Author Consulting

On-site professional learning with sustainable results! Let us help you design a professional learning plan to meet the unique needs of your school or district. www.corwin.com/pd

Institutes

Institutes

Corwin Institutes provide collaborative learning experiences that equip your team with tools and action plans ready for immediate implementation. www.corwin.com/institutes

eCourses

eCourses

Practical, flexible online professional learning designed to let you go at your own pace. www.corwin.com/ecourses

Read2Earn

Read2Earn

Did you know you can earn graduate credit for reading this book? Find out how: www.corwin.com/read2earn